CW01500755

Contents

Why Atmosphere, Discipline, and Life?

My journey with the Charlotte Mason educational philosophy began when my first child was just a baby. I clicked on an article about homeschooling, and several clicks later, landed on a blog about a British woman who trained teachers at a college in the English Lake District over 100 years ago. Before long, I became fascinated by this woman, Charlotte Mason, and the impact her ideas still have today. As a result, my husband and I never actively made a decision to homeschool. We simply thought and spoke about it for so long that it became the only real option.

I began to read blogs and books about education, homeschooling, and Charlotte Mason. As I sifted through the myriad resources on the Charlotte Mason way, including Charlotte Mason's own published works, I realized that much of her philosophy's beauty lies in its ability to avoid prescriptive, dogmatic answers to complex questions and challenging situations. In her own words, she gives us a method of education that embraces the individuality of children, rather than a prescriptive, one-size-fits-all system.[1]

The Charlotte Mason philosophy is much more than a curriculum. It's not a list of 'do's and 'don't's, or a series of items on a to-do list. And while it might sound nice to be told exactly what to do in order to give

---

[1] Charlotte Mason, *Home Education*, (Living Book Press, 2017), 9.

AMY FISCHER

Before Curriculum

How to Start Practicing the Charlotte Mason
Philosophy in your Home

our children a Charlotte Mason education, we actually have something much better: a set of principles that we use to set our focus, inform our choices, and apply this beautiful, rich philosophy in any context.

An Education Based on Principles

Using the Charlotte Mason philosophy starts with understanding the principles behind it. Charlotte Mason herself tells us of the importance of this. In her sixth volume, she says,

> *I feel strongly that to attempt to work this method without a firm adherence to the few principles laid down would be not only idle but disastrous. "Oh, we could do anything with books like those," said a master; he tried the books and failed conspicuously because he ignored the principles.*[2]

No one wants their homeschool to be a disaster. We don't want to be idle, and we don't want to fail. But in order to avoid calamity, we need to turn our attention to a few fundamental ideas.

Charlotte Mason distilled her philosophy into twenty principles, and she wrote six books and countless articles explaining, illustrating, and expanding on them. If we include the articles in the magazine she edited in her lifetime and the numerous books, articles, and blogs *about* her philosophy, we can quickly become overwhelmed. We all have full lives and schedules. We need a jumping off point that will allow us to actively practice the Charlotte Mason method while we learn more about it.

---

[2]   Charlotte Mason, *An Essay Towards a Philosophy of Education*, (Living Book Press, 2017), 270.

With this in mind, I have focused this book on Charlotte Mason's motto, 'Education is an atmosphere, a discipline, and a life'.[3] In her philosophy, she refers to these as the three instruments or tools that we use in the education of our children. I will explore what each of these mean later in the book, but first, let's consider what makes these educational tools acceptable, and why other tools are off-limits.

The Starting Premise: Children are Born Persons

Charlotte Mason's first principle says, "Children are born persons".[4] While it is tempting to gloss over this idea, thinking, "of course a child is a *person*", this is not a passing comment and understanding this principle is very relevant to our daily practice of her philosophy.

By "children are born persons", Charlotte Mason means that children are born with everything they need in order to learn, including desire, ability, and motivation. Charlotte Mason believed that schools, teachers, and parents too often appealed to children's other desires in order to motivate learning.[5] Rewards for a good mark, punishments for a bad one, pressure to fit in with peers or to stand out among them. These are all examples of how we might disrespectfully encroach upon a child's personality. If a child is subject to these forces for too long, then these other desires may overpower and possibly destroy our child's inner motivation to learn.

In place of rewards and punishments, Charlotte Mason gives us the

<hr>

[3] Charlotte Mason's Twenty Principles, Principle 5, available at https://www.ambleside online.org/CM/20Principles.html

[4] Charlotte Mason's Twenty Principles, Principle 1.

[5] Mason, *Philosophy,* "The Sacredness of Personality", 80-93

tools of atmosphere, discipline, and life. These tools respect a child's personality and trust that a child desires for knowledge for its own sake. They do not prey upon a child's appetite for success, fame, fear of failure, or anything else.[6] We employ these tools from a place of trust: we trust that our children have the inner drive to learn, and that our job is *not* to cajole our kids into learning. As Charlotte Mason put it, our children are not oysters, and we are not in the business of stuffing them full of information.[7]

Atmosphere, discipline and life are the means to an education without carrots and sticks. If that's what you want for your children, this book - and the Charlotte Mason way - are for you.

* * *

If you would like an extra helping hand as you work your way through the principles of atmosphere, discipline, and life, I have a free workbook available at http://aroundthethicket.com/workbook. The sections in the workbook align with the chapters in this book and provide action-oriented prompts and questions so that you can better apply these concepts in your home.

---

[6]   Ibid.

[7]   Mason, *Philosophy*, 33.

I

Atmosphere

"When we say that 'education is an atmosphere,' we do not mean that a child should be isolated in what may be called a 'child-environment' especially adapted and prepared, but that we should take into account the educational value of his natural home atmosphere, both as regards persons and things, and should let him live freely among his proper conditions. It stultifies a child to bring down his world to the child's level."

Charlotte Mason's Sixth Principle

1

Atmosphere Starts with Us

E ducation is an *atmosphere*. Charlotte Mason uses this phrase to acknowledge that a significant part of a child's education comes from simply living life.[8] Playing with siblings, taking care of pets or plants, running errands, doing chores. Everything a child encounters has the opportunity to teach him or her about cooperation, responsibility, hard work, and countless other lessons. All of these situations, people, obstacles, and successes contribute to the atmosphere in which a child grows up.

Our children breath in atmosphere like air. They are constantly taking it in, and learning from it, without realizing it. Yet, while it exerts an immense influence upon our children, it's easy to think that we have little to no control over the atmosphere of our homes. It feels too abstract. However, if we ignore atmosphere, we ignore an immense portion of how our children are educated. I think we can actively cultivate a home atmosphere that helps our kids become self-motivated learners, and, eventually, responsible adults. That's what we'll explore in this chapter

---

[8] Mason, *Philosophy*, 94.

and the next.

To begin, we need to acknowledge that a significant part of our home atmosphere begins with *ourselves,* the parents. Charlotte Mason founded and edited a magazine called the *Parents' Review,* which published an article in 1897 called 'The Atmosphere of the Home'.[9] Let's consider some of the key points.

Authentic Faith Establishes an Authentic Atmosphere

First, the article discusses the role that our faith plays in our home atmosphere. The article states:

> *The test will be whether religion is the centre of our life, the joy of our joy, the consolation of our sorrow, the one eminently important thing for which all others have to give way; whether we view the things of daily life primarily with reference to it, and whether all else is felt to be relatively devoid of interest and value.*[10]

Our children will feel the effects of our faith more than anyone else. They are the people who will know whether Christ really is the king over our lives, or whether we are living in hypocrisy. They are the ones who will see if our actions line up with our words. Is church just something for Sunday mornings, or do they see us walking in our faith throughout the week?

Our children need to see our faith - to see and hear us read our Bibles and

---

[9] M.F. Jerrod, "The Atmosphere of the Home", *The Parents' Review,* (Ambleside, Parents' National Educational Union, 1897), 772-777.

[10] Ibid.

pray, to hear conversations about seeking God's will, to know how we are applying Scripture to our lives. In the book of Joshua, God's people build a monument when they enter the Promised Land, specifically so that when children ask about it, their parents remember to tell them of God's great power and faithfulness to His people.[11] What monuments are we building in our homes, our routines, our daily lives that inspire our childrens' curiosity, and allow us to share God's love, power, and faithfulness with our children in a natural way?

An Eternal Perspective Keeps Relationships Healthy

Second, the article asks us to consider whether we are building a home atmosphere that allows our children to be authentic and real with us. It says,

> Little trivialities of manner or expression, the way of talking which is not just what we should have wished, the choice that is not just the one we should like to have seen made, we must learn to pass these things over as the trifles they are, otherwise there is an end to all freedom, and, what is more serious, an end of reality. Our children may then learn to be the thing we wish in our presence, but they will be themselves still, they will have their own idiosyncrasies, their own individuality, but unknown and unknowable to us. So much for the larger outlook.[12]

Our children have minds of their own. After all, they are persons! Naturally, they will have their own opinions, make their own choices, and frankly, do things that we simply wouldn't do ourselves. The question

---

[11] Joshua Chapter 4, specifically v. 21-22.

[12] Jerrod, "Atmosphere".

is, 'Does it really matter?'

If our hearts are focused on eternity, if our desire is to see our children fit for the service of our Father, then there are many, many details of their lives that simply are not worth our judgement or comment. For example, whether my child chooses to wear matching socks, which book from our shelf he chooses to read in his free time, which musical instrument or sport she learns to play, and so on, these are ultimately trivialities. I do my child a severe disservice if I choose to assert my opinion on him.

When we nitpick the details, we are creating an atmosphere that tells our children that their individuality doesn't matter - conformity with our vision does. As our children pick up on these clues, they, as the quote states, stop showing us who they really are. They start to present a pretend version of themselves - either one that tries to make us (rather than their heavenly Father) happy, or one that tries to establish their autonomy in more significant and drastic ways.

Let us keep ourselves out of God's place in the lives of our children - if our personal goal is to live life with Him at the centre, then surely we should have the same goal for our children. And that requires letting trifles be trifles, and allowing them to pass without comment.

Our Values Inform the Atmosphere

Finally, let's consider values. The article says,

> When our children grow up and go out to see many sorts of manners, and many different standards of conduct, one of their safeguards will be in the idea they have formed of what is worth-while. Pleasure and success and admiration—they will want all

these, and to almost every one of them some small triumphs will be given, and whether these are sufficient will depend on what they are accustomed to seeing valued. Let us then covet one gift for our children, that of unworldliness.[13]

Charlotte Mason wrote that people, which includes children, have all sorts of appetites.[14] We have desires to fit in with others, to succeed in life, to be happy and successful, to please other people. These desires are not necessarily bad in and of themselves. The trouble comes when these desires are our only motivation, and the trajectory of our lives moves in order to secure worldly success. If in word and action, we show our children that money, success, power, and fame are the main goals worth attaining, our children will imbibe those values.

What ideas are we giving to our children about what is worthwhile? I think we find the answer to this question in two places.

First, how do we spend our time? If we are frenetically busy and have very little space in our lives for rest, that reflects our values. Likewise, if we consistently neglect our responsibilities, that also shows our children what is important. All of us face busy times of life, and times where we have less on our plate, but ultimately it is good to aim for an appropriate balance between work and rest.

Second, how do we motivate our children? Charlotte Mason felt that to use rewards or punishments to get our children to learn was an infringement on their personality.[15] This includes comparing our

---

[13] Ibid.

[14] Charlotte Mason, *Ourselves*, (Living Book Press, 2017)

[15] Charlotte Mason's Twenty Principles, Principle 4.

children to others, suggesting that 'studying hard will help them get ahead in life', or 'failing to learn this now means you won't get a job later'. All of these attitudes tacitly tell our children that worldly success is the purpose of learning and that it is worth striving for.

Rather than rewards or punishments, Charlotte Mason believed that we should protect and nourish a child's appetite for learning by feeding it appropriately - on living ideas and much knowledge, an idea I will discuss in Chapter 5.[16] Children don't need to be manipulated to learn. By using atmosphere, discipline and life, we avoid manipulation and let children learn because they have a natural, inner drive to do so.

Our Home Atmosphere can Rest in Grace

There is no easy tip or trick to get atmosphere right. And in fact, we will often get it very, very wrong. But that is no reason to despair or give up. In fact, I believe that failure, and our response to it, is a beautiful, hopeful part of atmosphere.

We are not raising perfect children to live in a perfect world. When our children are grown and they leave the nest, they aren't going to be living in community with perfect people. Learning to live with parents who fall short prepares them to live with friends, spouses, and children who fall short.

Our children will take in our responses to our own failures, and use their observations to form their own values. When we fail and then repent, we show our children that humility is of greater importance than our reputation. We speak volumes about our values when we are willing to

---

[16] Charlotte Mason's Twenty Principles, Principle 9.

say that we are wrong, and our children see us turn away from sin.

Ultimately, our home atmosphere hinges on our attitudes: our attitudes towards our faith, our attitudes towards our children, our attitudes towards earthly rewards. To use atmosphere effectively, the most important thing we can do is to grow our own faith and develop our ability to humbly look at our lives, our children, our work, and even our failures, from the perspective of eternity.

I'd like to leave you with one final quote from the Parent's Review article that illustrates the powerful opportunity we have to give our children a fruitful home atmosphere:

> *If we have understood noble things; if we have felt and acted as though nobleness were the one thing worth being and having; if through sordidness and worldliness, we have sought out and be-lieved in pure motives...then, I say that our children are breathing an atmosphere which is verily life-giving, and that mean aims and low motives will be to them destruction and not delight.*[17]

---

[17] Jerrod, "Atmosphere".

2

The Art of Masterly Inactivity

I n the last chapter, I wrote largely about our own attitudes, and how they influence the atmosphere of our homes. Growing and improving our home atmosphere from this perspective is largely about growing in our own faith and taking an eternal perspective on what is happening around us. But while this aspect of atmosphere centers on our relationship with God, another aspect of atmosphere centers on our relationship with our children.

While we all bring a unique approach to parenting, we are all influenced by broad cultural movements. In recent years, that cultural movement has been 'helicopter parenting'.[18] This phenomenon refers to parents who hover over their children constantly, solving every problem their children face. They pick up the pieces of their child's every failure, to the point of calling university professors to demand better grades.

_____

[18] e.g. Sandi Schwartz, "Helicopter Parenting", *The Gottman Institute*, (2018), available at https://www.gottman.com/blog/helicopter-parenting-good-intentions-poor-outcomes/.

Sadly, this type of parenting often makes children very unhappy, and lowers - instead of increases - their chances for success in life. Children who have every obstacle removed on their behalf never build up the strength to face their own challenges. Children who never fail don't learn that setbacks are a part of life, and that it is possible - and normal - to dust yourself off after falling and continue moving along. Children are becoming more anxious because they feel that their lives are out of their control. The healthy sense of autonomy that they started to develop as stubborn two-year-olds was stunted.[19]

Hyper-intensive Parenting Affects Us All

It's easy to hear of these more extreme examples and to think, 'I would never do a thing like that to my child'. However, culture impacts us without us realizing it. That's what makes it culture.

How have we been impacted by the culture of hyper intensive parenting? The answer doesn't lie in what we wish to be true, but in our parenting choices, actions, and reactions. For example, how do we respond when our children face difficult challenges? What about when they are on the brink of failure or even when they do *not* succeed? How do we react when our children want to deviate from the path that we think best for their future success?

If we parent out of fear, anxiety, or a desire to control our children's lives, even if we believe it is for their best, then we are growing a home atmosphere of fear and control. It hardly needs to be said that this is not a healthy environment for children. What we need is an alternative to the cultural norm. We need an approach to parenting that is rooted in

---

[19] William Stixrud and Ned Johnson, *The Thriving Child*, (Penguin, 2018).

faith and gives our children freedom within age-appropriate boundaries. Charlotte Mason calls this approach 'masterly inactivity'.[20]

An Atmosphere of Masterly Inactivity

Charlotte Mason believed that atmosphere prepares children for real life in the real world by allowing them to live life in the real world. As they grow up, children will naturally come against challenges, adversity, setbacks, frustrations, denied wishes, and elusive goals. While this may be difficult to watch as a parent, these situations allow our children to develop resilience and grit, and to grow their character. If we prevent our children from facing these situations, we prevent development of qualities that are necessary to their future success and happiness.[21]

Charlotte Mason refers to masterly inactivity as a 'wise letting-alone'. We allow our children to face their own obstacles, and resist the temptation to smooth every difficulty and help them over every hurdle. Masterly inactivity is the art of knowing when to get involved in our children's lives, and the wisdom of knowing that our involvement is probably not required as often as we think. Charlotte Mason says in School Education, "[Masterly Inactivity] indicates the power to act, the desire to act, and the insight and self-restraint which forbid action."[22]

I'd like to give one caveat before we continue. Masterly inactivity is not the practice of letting our children do whatever they want, allowing them to enter into situations that are truly dangerous, or of needlessly

---

[20] Charlotte Mason, *School Education*, "Masterly Inactivity", (Living Book Press, 2017), 25-35.

[21] Ibid.

[22] Ibid., 28.

burdening our children with our emotions or details about challenges we face that are inappropriate for their age or stage. The wisdom of masterly inactivity requires us to use our knowledge of our children to know whether a particular circumstance would be educational for our children and would grow their strength and character, or whether it would do lasting harm.

Practicing Masterly Inactivity in your Home

So where do we start with masterly inactivity? Charlotte Mason gives us several qualities to consider, but first, she starts with the concept of 'authority'.[23] To let our children alone without a sense of our authority over them gives our children license to do whatever they want. Most, if not all, children are deeply affected when they lack a safe, secure authority in their life. Even though children push boundaries, they are comforted to find that they are there, confidently enforced by us.[24]

When my children were very little, I put a lot of effort into creating safe play spaces for them. I gated off a room, got rid of anything dangerous, and bolted the furniture to the wall. I knew that if I was locked out of the house while my child was in that room, he would be perfectly safe when I got back in - hungry and upset, perhaps, but no real lasting harm.

Authority is like those baby gates: my children could push and pull at the gate for ages, but could not move them. Within the boundaries, however, they had freedom to play what they chose, when they chose. We need to

---

[23] Ibid., 33.

[24] E.g. Janet Lansbury, "The Real Reason Toddlers Push Limits", *Elevating Childcare*, (2013), available at https://www.janetlansbury.com/2013/10/the-real-reasons-toddlers-push-limits/.

take this same attitude and apply it to whatever stage our children are in. As parents we establish and enforce boundaries, but our children have room within those limits to exercise their freedom. To use Charlotte Mason's terms, we balance 'letting-alone' with wise, enforced limits and boundaries.

Herein lies the challenge for us. Charlotte Mason says,

> *Parents and teachers must, of course, be omniscient; their children expect this of them, and a mother or father who can be hoodwinked is a person easy to reckon with in the mind of even the best child. For children are always playing a game--half of chance, half of skill; they are trying how far they can go, how much of the management of their own lives they can get for the taking, and how much they must leave in the hands of the stronger powers. Therefore the mother who is not up to children is at their mercy, and need expect no quarter. But she must see without watching, know without telling, be on the alert always, yet never obviously, fussily, so. This open-eyed attitude must be sphinx-like in its repose.*[25]

Masterly inactivity starts with knowing - knowing our children, appreciating their ages and stages, acting calmly as our children push the limits, and ensuring that the limits move when our children are ready.

Parenting by Faith

Masterly inactivity also requires an attitude of trust - trust in ourselves, in our children, and in God. Charlotte Mason writes,

---

[25] Mason, *School Education*, 30-31.

Parents should trust themselves more. Everything is not done by restless endeavour. The mere blessed fact of the parental relationship and of that authority which belongs to it, by right and by nature, acts upon the children as do sunshine and shower on a seed in good soil.[26]

Children feel secure when their relationship with their parents is rooted in faith about their future, rather than anxiety.[27] Ultimately, hyper-intensive parenting is about needlessly taking control of our children's lives because we are overwhelmed by the possible consequences of their circumstances, choices, and actions today. Masterly inactivity, to the contrary, challenges us to set aside concerns that our children will miss out on scholarships, career opportunities, or worldly success by not taking the right path now. We do not need to orchestrate our children's lives for success. Rather, we appreciate that doing so will rob our children of many character building and strengthening experiences that will support them in the future.

Ultimately, masterly inactivity, and using atmosphere as an educational tool, is an act of faith. By faith we trust that while we love our children, God loves them more. He will allow situations and circumstances to come their way that He will use to grow them into the people He wants them to be. While it is hard to see our kids struggle and even fail, while we may feel like we need to do more to educate our kids, we recognize that even though we can only see a small part of the plan, we are more often called to 'be still and know'[28] rather than anxiously intervene.

---

[26] Ibid., 29.

[27] Stixrud and Johnson, *Thriving.*

[28] Psalm 46:10

II

Discipline

"By 'education is a discipline,' we mean the discipline of habits, formed definitely and thoughtfully, whether habits of mind or body."
Charlotte Mason's Seventh Principle

3

Why Habit Training?

“**E**ducation is a discipline”. For some, this invokes ideas of a perfectly structured and scheduled homeschool day, executed with punctuality, precision, and perfection. For most, if not all of us, that image is unattainable and completely unrealistic. Fortunately, what Charlotte Mason refers to with this tool is the discipline of *habit*, “formed definitely and thoughtfully whether habits of mind or of body”.[29]

Habit training is a buzzing topic, especially in Charlotte Mason circles. I think we can all imagine how nice it would be to have children who don't have to be told constantly what to do and when to do it. We would love children who do the right thing out of habit, and not because we ask, remind, or nag them. We even wish we could be the same! But although we have a vision for where habit training could take us, many of us, including myself, aren't sure where to start, and experience a fair share of frustration in figuring it out.

---

[29] Charlotte Mason's Twenty Principles, Principle 7.

As we dig into habit training, let's begin by considering why we do it in the first place. Why is habit training an instrument of education?

Our Habits Form our Character

Habit training is the balancing force to masterly inactivity. While masterly inactivity lets our children alone in wisdom, habit training is intentional 'interference' on our part. If the practice of masterly inactivity allows our children to learn through life as it comes, with our quiet support in the background, then habit training happens when we, the parents, need to intervene.[30]

But why would we interfere? Charlotte Mason has much to say about this, but our overarching goal is to help our children to develop a good character. Charlotte Mason writes,

> [The child] depends upon his parents; it rests with them to initiate the thoughts he shall think, the desires he shall cherish, the feelings he shall allow. Only to initiate; no more is permitted to them; but from this initiation will result the habits of thought and feeling which govern the man--his character, that is to say.[31]

As parents, we have a profound influence upon our children. Whether we like it or not, the atmosphere of our homes constantly informs our children's actions, thoughts, and feelings. But leaving these qualities completely to atmosphere and to the child's own nature is shortsighted. Charlotte Mason implores us to not leave our child's character to chance, but use the tool of habit training to intentionally nourish and develop

---

[30] Mason, *Home Education*, 104.

[31] Ibid., 109.

it.[32]

Habits are Inevitable

This brings us to the second reason we habit train - everyone has habits, for better or worse. While our children's thoughts and actions are shaped both by their home atmosphere and their nature, they are strengthened by habit. The more our children think or behave along a certain line, the stronger their tendency grows to repeat that thought or behavior. The action compounds. The longer the habit is maintained, the greater its effect. Charlotte Mason says,

> *Habit is inevitable. If we fail to ease life by laying down habits of right thinking and right acting, habits of wrong thinking and wrong acting fix themselves of their own accord.*[33]

Habits establish themselves on a physiological level - neurologically, every time we repeat an action, the relevant pathway between neurons fires and grows stronger. This is how deeply we are influenced by our habits: they embed themselves within our very brain structure.[34]

Our children are constantly in the process of forming habits. Consequently, we should be motivated to help our children form the best ones. We want this not for our own sake, but because we appreciate that their lives will go more smoothly when they have better habits.

This is an important distinction to make. Habit training respects a child's

---

[32] Ibid., 102-103.

[33] Mason, *Philosophy*, 101.

[34] Mason, *Home Education*, "The Physiology of Habit", 111-118.

personality. It is not coercive or manipulative – and crucially, we are not trying to conform our children to our own idea of how they should behave. Habit training must start from a position of humility, and considering the child's needs before our own convenience. We should not take lightly the influence we bear on our children's lives.

Ideas Make the Foundation of Habit Training

When we have a vision for why we habit train, the next question is where to start. Charlotte Mason has plenty to say on this point, although I will discuss the 'nuts and bolts' application of habit training in the next chapter.

Charlotte Mason tells us that habit training begins with the inspiration of an idea.[35] Whether it's something we read in a book, or a spark of insight we have into our children's lives, we need to have an initial awareness of where we need to focus our habit training efforts. This idea needs to be shared with our children. Charlotte Mason says,

> We must sow the idea or notion which makes the act [of the habit] worthwhile.[36]

Our ability to appreciate the impact of our children's habits on their characters relies on the ideas we take in and give attention to. Ideas help us imagine the future and can inspire us to develop good habits and conquer vices, both in ourselves and in our children. We will return to this discussion of ideas in Part III. At the moment, we need to recognize that habit training does not happen in a vacuum. We need the input of

---

[35] Mason, *Philosophy*, 102.

[36] Ibid.

ideas, examples, and especially, the Holy Spirit.

Habit Training is Immediately Applicable

Even before we are ready to start training our children in a new habit, we have many areas where we can bring our active effort. To begin, we can start preventing bad habits straight away. The more bad habits we can stop in their tracks, the fewer ingrained bad habits we will need to replace with good habits. More effort now means much less effort in the long run.[37]

I believe one of the best things we can do is to stop our children in the middle of the bad habit - as quickly as possible - and ask them to practice the good habit in its place. We don't need to punish our children for their bad habits. Instead, when we see them starting the habit, we can stop them, and ask them to practice the good habit instead.

Practicing has lots of benefits. First, it puts us in a position of *helping* our children. We are on their team, we want them to get it right, and we are committed to cheering them through. Second, practicing strengthens the neural pathways of the *right* action. Research has even shown that just by asking a child to *imagine* doing an activity, they strengthen the neural pathways for doing that activity again in the future.[38]

What might it look like to stop a bad habit in action and require our children to practice?

---

[37] e.g. Charlotte Mason, *Formation of Character*, "Ability", (Living Books Press 2017), 89-98.

[38] Daniel J. Siegel and Tina Payne Bryson, *No Drama Discipline*, (London, Scribe, 2014).

- For a toddler about to hit their sibling, you might gently catch their hand and say, 'I won't let you hit'.
- If your child is whining or shouting for something, you might tell them, 'Please try asking again. Practice using your best, nicest voice'.
- For an older child, it might look like asking them to re-do a chore because their first effort just wasn't up to snuff.

These are only a few examples, and I'm sure you can think of many more relevant to your own children. In general, though, allowing our children to 're-do' a bad habit the correct way is a non-punitive approach to dealing with misbehavior that also establishes good habits.

Choosing the First Habit

While we are on guard against bad habits, habit training is not just reactionary. We also need to cultivate good habits. Charlotte Mason mentions many habits within her works, but if choosing from a long list of possible good habits sounds daunting, you are not alone. I recommend narrowing down the options in a few ways.

First, think about your day and where points of tension flare up in your home. Try to imagine one, simple change you could make that would ease up this tension and help your day go more smoothly. It might be tidying up toys before bed, helping get dinner ready, or, for us, having our children get dressed at a regular time each day. Choosing a habit that resolves tension will improve our home atmosphere - which means we are using two of Charlotte Mason's educational tools at once. Plus, the benefits will be encouraging because they will be noticeable and even quantifiable. Success will help motivate us to continue on.

Second, start with a concrete habit. Charlotte Mason suggests establishing all sorts of habits with our children, including the habits of attention, self-control, and integrity.[39] These are extremely important habits, but they are more difficult to conceptualize than habits like washing hands, getting dressed, and making the bed. We certainly need to give consideration to the more abstract habits, and invest time in them, but if you're new to habit training, then I think it is worth starting with habits that are tangible.

Third, choose a habit that you know you can enforce. Choosing a concrete habit helps with this - it's easy to see if a child has tidied up their toys. You might also choose a habit that doesn't require us to inspect their work more often than we can manage. A habit like making the bed happens once a day, which means that you will need to put on your habit training hat *once* each day in order to make sure the habit has happened. This makes it a less intensive habit than your child putting toys away when he is finished with them. That is a habit you need to watch over the whole day. Again, this isn't to say that we never dive into habits that require more regular vigilance on our part. This is a suggestion to help you get a gentle, successful start to habit training that you can build on for more complex habits.

When we have a vision for habit training, and the "smooth and easy days" that Charlotte Mason says it will bring, it is tempting to dive in to the deep end.[40] For some, this may be the right place to start. But for many of us, including myself, plunging in has meant avoidance on the one hand, and finding myself in over my head on the other. By thoughtfully choosing the first few habits to train our children in, we can make the

---

[39] e.g. Mason, *Home Education*, "Infant 'Habits'", 124-132.

[40] Mason, *Home Education*, 136.

task less overwhelming and more successful. In light of the big picture, this is often the best place to start.

4

The Nuts and Bolts of Habits

C hoosing a habit to help your children build is the initial step towards using 'discipline' as a tool of education. In order to continue, we need to understand how a habit actually works, so that we can prepare accordingly. Fortunately, a lot of research on habits has happened since Charlotte Mason was living and writing - work that brings clarity and simplicity to our understanding of habits and how we can make habit training work in our homes.

The first idea we need to consider is that habits have four parts: cue, craving, response, reward. Author James Clear discusses these in detail in his book. *Atomic Habits*.[41] It is an excellent resource, but for our purposes, I'll summarize some of the most pertinent points.

Habit Cues

Every habit starts with a signal, or a 'cue', that tells us to perform the habit. You are probably aware of some of your own habit cues. Locking

---

[41] James Clear, *Atomic Habits*, (Random House Business, 2018).

the front door might initiate the habit of hanging up your keys. Coming into the kitchen in the morning initiates the habit of filling and boiling the kettle. Children running through the kitchen initiates the habit of telling them to 'shut the door'.

When we start habit training, it's essential that we determine what the cue for our habit is going to be. If we don't have a solid, reliable cue, we will only haphazardly complete our habits. In fact, we won't really establish a new habit at all, because we won't be learning to do something on autopilot.

What will be the signal that initiates the new habit? Ideally, you will choose something simple, like leaving or entering a room, finishing a meal, or closing a book. You'll need to look for a cue that happens consistently, and with the same regularity as you wish the habit to be performed. For example, coming indoors would be a great cue to wash hands after playing outside. Every time a child plays outside, he or she will come indoors. Therefore, the cue takes place *every* time you want the habit performed.

In our family, we read aloud after breakfast every day. We call this our 'morning basket'. We also have a habit of getting dressed after we finish reading. We only read from our morning basket once a day, and my kids only need to get dressed once a day. The occurrence of the cue matches the number of times I need the behavior to take place. This makes it an appropriate cue for the habit.

Habit Cravings

Let's look at 'craving' next. You might be familiar with the scientist Pavlov and his dogs. Pavlov regularly fed his dogs a treat every time he rang a bell. Quickly, the dogs associated the sound of the bell with receiving a treat. Before long, just hearing the bell was enough for the dogs to start salivating, expectantly awaiting a treat, even if there was none in sight. The sound of the bell initiated the dogs' *craving* for the tasty *reward* of a dog treat.[42]

A cue doesn't directly initiate an action - it prompts a craving for the reward received after the action has been completed. I'll talk a bit more about the role of rewards in habit training, and about choosing the right rewards, but for now, we need to know that habits are more than mechanical action. There is a reward in place that motivates the behavior. In order to get that craving going, we need to have an understanding of the reward our children will receive for the habit.

Habit Responses

The part of a habit that gets the most attention is 'response'. This is the *actual* behavior that we want to see our children carry out. As you think through the new habit, you might consider a few questions: is it appropriate for me to expect this of my child? Can I clearly communicate it in a way my child understands? Does it fit within their maturity and physical ability? Do I need to make accommodations or adjust anything in my home in order to make it possible for my child to complete this action ? Do I need to get a stepstool so they can reach the sink? A

---

[42] Saul McLeod, "Pavlov's Dogs", *Simple Psychology*, (2018), available at https://www.simplypsychology.org/pavlov.html

picture chart so they can remember all the steps? Different storage so that my child can successfully put toys away? An adjustment to my schedule, so my child has time to finish their tasks? If our expectations are inappropriate, then our habit training endeavor will soon crumble, as well as our kids and our patience.

Habit Rewards

The habit cycle ends with 'reward'. Reward is the resolution of the craving and the completion of a habit. Rewards can go two directions. They can be external to our child - prizes, money, praise from parents or a sense of doing better than others, like their siblings. Rewards can also be internal, intrinsic to the child.

Using external rewards does not align with the Charlotte Mason philosophy. Charlotte Mason felt that using these external motivators oversteps the limits of parental authority, and manipulates a child's personality.[43] External motivators are likely to nurture aspects of a child's character that would be better left alone - traits like ambition, desire for approval, and comparison to others. As she writes in Philosophy of Education,

> Each such desire has its place but the results are disastrous if any one should dominate.[44]

The warning here is this: if we use external motivators, we are raising children who will not only come to rely on them, but who will have an appetite for these rewards beyond what they ought.

---

[43] Charlotte Mason's Twenty Principles, Principle 4.

[44] Mason, *Philosophy*, 88.

Natural Rewards for Habits

Without these options, how are our children rewarded for their good habits? Charlotte Mason writes,

> For a habit is a delight in itself; poor human nature is conscious of the ease that it is to repeat the doing of anything without effort; and, therefore, the formation of a habit, the gradually lessening sense of effort in a given act, is pleasurable.[45]

As habits get easier, our children will find a natural reward: the sense of doing something easily. The fact that they need less effort to choose to do something, and that they are doing it without thinking – that is a reward in itself. The *craving* becomes a desire for the resolution of a job well done and the peace of a clear conscience. We may also find intrinisic rewards that are specific to the habit. These could include the feeling of personal cleanliness, pride in taking care of oneself and one's home, and so on.

Ultimately, a natural reward occurs when our children have fulfilled a duty and are now free to fill their time as they see fit – within our limits, of course. This brings us to another reward that Charlotte Mason mentions in her writing – the natural reward of 'free time'. A child's spare time should not necessarily be used to ask for more from the child. Charlotte Mason writes,

> Now, rewards should be dealt out to the child upon principle: they should be the natural consequences of his good conduct. What is the natural consequence of work well and quickly done? Is it not

---

[45] Mason, *Home Education*, 121.

the enjoyment of ampler leisure?[46]

We can bear this in mind when considering the 'reward' part of a habit: that leisure time is a wonderful reward for completing a habit that does not play upon a child's personality.

We may not be able to tell at the beginning what our children will find motivating – but the key principle is that we trust to these inner rewards rather than external rewards.

Setting a New Habit in Motion

Establishing a new habit starts with speaking with our child. When we talk with our child about a new habit, Charlotte Mason encourages us to speak to our child as their "friendly ally".[47] We want to speak to our child as teammates, which doesn't include giving lectures. The purpose of this chat is to make our expectations clear. They need to know the cue, what behavior is expected, and what is on the other side of that habit, waiting as a reward.

After this, it's time to go into action. Our responsibility is to ensure the habit takes place after every cue, and to guard that habit, even when we think that a habit is firmly cemented in. Perseverance and watchfulness are challenging, especially when we have multiple children, a home to look after, and homeschooling responsibilities.[48]

We can take heart, though. Charlotte Mason says that habit training in

---

[46] Ibid., 143.

[47] Ibid., 123.

[48] Ibid., 122.

itself becomes a habit.[49] We can expect ourselves to find increasing ease in habit training, in the vigilance that is required. We can find pleasure when we fulfill our calling, in exercising this valuable educational tool, and in serving our children in this way. It is tempting to give up, to let things slide. But be encouraged. We moms need the discipline of good habits, too – and it is a worthwhile pursuit.

[49] Ibid., 136.

III

Life

"In saying that 'education is a life,' the need of intellectual and moral as well as of physical sustenance is implied. The mind feeds on ideas, and therefore children should have a generous curriculum."
Charlotte Mason's Eighth Principle

5

Living Books for Living Minds

I n order to understand how 'education is a life', we have to understand a basic metaphor in the Charlotte Mason philosophy: our mind is like our body. In order to sustain life and growth, our minds, like our bodies, need to be fed an appropriate diet.[50]

For our bodies, this is fairly straightforward. We need a varied diet, plenty of fruit and vegetables, and not too many sweets. We also need rest and exercise. But what about our minds? Charlotte Mason summarizes the answer to this question in her ninth principle:

> *We hold that the child's mind is no mere sac to hold ideas; but is rather, if the figure may be allowed, a spiritual organism, with an appetite for all knowledge. This is its proper diet, with which it is prepared to deal; and which it can digest and assimilate as the body does foodstuffs.*[51]

---

[50] Charlotte Mason's Twenty Principles, Principle 8.

[51] Ibid., Principle 9.

The proper diet, the correct food for our minds, is *knowledge*, and Charlotte Mason tells us that our children feed on knowledge when they are put in touch with *ideas*. Not only that, but our children have an appetite for *all* knowledge. Just like our children need to eat a variety of foods to stay healthy, so they need encounter a wide variety of ideas.

An Education Based on Principles

Principles are the key to making philosophy applicable. For example, even though I'm not an expert on child nutrition, I know a few nutritional principles that help me give my children a healthy diet. In the same way, I can offer my children a healthy diet of ideas, simply by understanding and applying a few basic principles.

This is the mindset we need in order to use 'life' as an educational tool. We need to know the principles: what kind of knowledge is wholesome for a child and how children take in that knowledge. When we know the answers to these questions, we can apply the principles within our own families. We don't have to worry that we're doing something different than the homeschooling family next door (or in our Facebook group or in our Instagram feed). In fact, we *expect* differences, just as we expect differences in the way we approach our children's diets.

What are the basic principles that we apply in order to ensure our children's minds are able to live and grow, just as their bodies? Charlotte Mason tells us that we need to provide our children with living books, on broad and varied topics. We must also trust our children to do the work of taking ideas from their books. Finally, we need to limit twaddle, a phrase for low-quality books that I will discuss later in this chapter.

Living Ideas are found in Living Books

First, we need to appreciate where our children can find ideas that will help their minds grow. One of the best sources of ideas for our children to 'consume' are found in living books. These are books that are well written and of literary quality. They inspire thought and meditation. Living books are not preachy, trying to get across a single moralistic point. In general, they *show* rather than *tell* our children many principles and ideas worthy of their attention. Living books should be the staple of our children's diet.[52]

Additionally, our children are able to tell the narratives back to us. This might happen in a conversation with them, in their play, or in a drawing. If we are doing formal lessons with our children, we might ask explicitly for a narration, when the child recounts the reading to us. If a child is able to retell a narrative in their own words, this is a good sign that they have read a living book.[53]

Children Require Broad and Varied Knowledge

A second principle that helps us choose books for our children is that, like the food we eat, children need a broad and varied diet for their minds. This means that they are put in touch with ideas from all areas of knowledge.[54] Charlotte Mason believed that this was the birthright of every child. The thought of putting our children in touch with an infinite amount of knowledge may be overwhelming. However, Charlotte Mason

---

[52] Mason, *School Education*, 162.

[53] Ibid., "How to Use Schoolbooks", 177-181.

[54] Mason, *Philosophy*, 235.

divided knowledge into three categories.[55] We can use these categories to check that our children are learning broadly.

- **The knowledge of God.** This almost speaks for itself. The knowledge of God is found in the ultimate living book - the Bible. This also includes theology.
- **The knowledge of man.** In this domain, we include literature, history, citizenship, languages, art.
- **The knowledge of the universe.** This is where we find science, geography, and mathematics.[56]

I don't believe it is necessary to make a checklist of all these subjects and attempt to loop through them on a regular basis. This would be like making a checklist of all the vegetables at the grocery store, and cycling through them without consideration of the season or your tastes. Instead, the general principle is that as we curate books for our children, whether we are reading to our preschoolers or setting a curriculum for our high schoolers, we choose books that cover all three areas of knowledge, and within those areas, we aim for variety.

Children Must do the Work of Learning Themselves

This brings us to a third principle: we cannot take in ideas for our children. With living books, our goal is to spread a feast and call our children to the table. We cannot force our children to eat, and we cannot digest their food for them. They must be the ones to assimilate the ideas they take in.[57]

---

[55] Ibid., 254.

[56] Ibid.

[57] Mason, *School Education*, 179-181.

Charlotte Mason gives us several points of caution. First, we shouldn't try to 'pre-chew' their food for them. This means that we do not tell them what a reading means, break it down, or put it into a form that we think they will understand. Generally, we avoid using abridgments and paraphrases, whether our own or that of another person. While this is not a hard and fast rule, we need to be wary of watered down stories.[58]

Second, we accept that we cannot mandate which ideas our children will take away from their books. A living book will have lots of living ideas, but we cannot pick and choose which ones will resonate with our child. We need to resist the temptation to 'help' our children find the ideas we think they need. Too often, this results in us preaching at or lecturing our children.[59] Rather than inspiring them, they begrudge our interference. Instead, we trust that if we have chosen good books, our children will grow from the myriad ideas within them.

Avoid Twaddle, the Candy of Books

The fourth and final principle we need to remember when choosing books for our children relates to that other genre of books: twaddle. Twaddle is the candy of books: easy reading, no real plot, conflict, or tension. The characters never face complicated choices, or even develop as people. The books contain no inspiring thought. They are pure entertainment.[60]

Here again, we take our basic nutritional principles and apply them as we see fit. Some families allow a bit of candy at home, others not at all. Some families allow a treat at weekends, others only allow it on

---

[58] Ibid., 226.

[59] Ibid., 162.

[60] Ibid., 168.

special occasions. We find the same with twaddle. We can look at our children's diet of ideas and determine whether we are happy to allow them some twaddle at home, or just at the library, or not at all. When we see how twaddle fits into the idea of nutrition for the mind, we can consider what other families do, and ultimately decide what is right for our own families, without feeling that we are doing something wrong.

Bringing the Life of Education into Action

Using 'life' as an educational tool is as simple as reading great books with our children. We choose a broad variety of the best books, avoid twaddle, and trust that as our children encounter living ideas, their minds will learn and grow.

Sometimes, however, this is easier said than done. After all, life happens. As a starting point, we can make the most of times we already read with our children, and use those moments to read the best books we can find. If our children read on their own, give them living books to read to themselves. We can look for new times of day to incorporate reading - it might be a morning basket, a poetry tea-time, or an after dinner ritual of reading together before bed. Lever the discipline of habit: find a cue for reading, and enjoy the time together.

We all face barriers to spreading the feast for our children. Sometimes, we only have time to heat up soup for dinner. Likewise, sometimes we are limited in our access to books, frustrated by the amount of twaddle around us, and limited in time for reading. But as with feeding our families, that quick bowl of soup is still hearty and nutritious, even if it is a quick meal. Even when life doesn't seem to work in our favor, we need to remember the big picture: spreading the feast doesn't happen once and end forever. The little meals and snacks all add up to a wide and varied diet that is life-sustaining for our children.

6

Life Out-of-Doors

L iving books are an essential part of the Charlotte Mason philosophy - our children need the ideas in those books to feed and grow their minds. But books are not the only source of living ideas. In fact, Charlotte Mason writes that some of the best "intellectual food," particularly for young children, can be found in nature.

Nature is a source of infinite living ideas, gently stimulating our children towards observation, thought, and new knowledge.[61] Charlotte Mason was adamant that children develop personal relationships with the natural world, so that they might glean the riches of an out-of-doors life.[62]

Living Ideas found Outdoors

Throughout her writing, Charlotte Mason emphasizes the value of time in nature for children. The youngest children, she felt, should

---

[61] Mason, *Home Education*, 61.

[62] Ibid., 71.

have copious time outdoors to play and observe nature.[63] As children began formal school lessons, nature walks and nature journaling were a constant fixture on the syllabus.[64] Even trainee teachers at Charlotte Mason's school spent time in the observation and study of the natural world.[65] She writes,

> In Science, or rather, nature study, we attach great importance to recognition, believing that the power to recognise and name a plant or stone or constellation involves classification and includes a good deal of knowledge. To know a plant by its gesture and habitat, its time and its way of flowering and fruiting; a bird by its flight and song and its times of coming and going; to know when, year after year, you may come upon the redstart and the pied fly-catcher, means a good deal of interested observation, and of; at any rate, the material for science.[66]

Nature is dynamic, changing moment by moment, day by day, and season by season. As children spend time in nature, they amass copious amounts of knowledge without our direct effort. This knowledge is "intellectual food" for our children. They will grow off of it just as they grow off the ideas found in living books.[67]

---

[63] Ibid.

[64] Mason, *School Education*, 237.

[65] Essex Cholmondeley, *The Story of Charlotte Mason*, (Dent, 1960).

[66] Mason, *School Education*, 236.

[67] Mason, *Home Education*, 61.

Love of Nature Enriches Life

Beyond food for our children's minds, time outdoors also gives our children a foundation for a full, rich life. Charlotte Mason writes,

> ...a love of Nature, implanted so early that it will seem to them hereafter to have been born in them, will enrich their lives with pure interests, absorbing pursuits, health, and good humour.[68]

When our children spend time in nature, they are building a relationship with it. They get to know trees, animals, seasons, and weather in a personal way. This is not something we have to force. Instead, we foster this relationship by taking our children outside, and trusting that it will catch their interest and their hearts.

The Ideal of Time Outdoors

Whatever our children's ages, developing the habit of spending time together in nature is a wonderful way of living out the Charlotte Mason philosophy. However, this is also an area where it's essential to have a firm understanding of the principles, so that we aren't unduly concerned when other people do it differently.

Charlotte Mason recognized that getting children outdoors and into nature can be challenging. You might live in a city, you might be short on time, you might live in a climate that has extreme weather. Charlotte Mason felt that outdoor time for children was of so much importance, though, that she asked parents to consider an ideal - that children would

---

[68] Ibid., 71.

spend the better part of each day outdoors – and to strive for it.[69]

I think we all have little excuses that keep us indoors. I know I do. However, our goal is not to get outdoors at all costs. The goal is to pick apart the flimsy excuses from the valid reasons we stay indoors, and do *what we can* about those reasons, while appreciating that we simply may not be able to achieve the four to six hours outside that Charlotte Mason specifically recommends.

Discover Natural Areas Around You

The first step is to consider where you and your children can spend time out of doors. Think about what is available to you. When my eldest was very little, I put my address into Google Maps and looked for green spaces within walking distance of my house. Later, we went exploring the places I saw online, finding a lovely open field with space to run and a little thicket to explore – a perfect picnic spot that we returned to many times.

I've applied a similar process before long trips in the car, looking for places to stop that would allow us to spend our lunch break out in the countryside rather than at crowded motorway services.

It's worth investing time in searching out places for your family to retreat to nature. And of course, don't overlook your own backyard!

---

[69] Ibid., 42.

Determine the Good and Bad Reasons that Keep You Indoors

The second step is to consider what prevents you from heading out to these places. Try to separate the reasonable from the superficial. Do you have all the right clothing? Does it take too long to gather what you need for the day? Charlotte Mason would have us know that it is *worth* the effort to do something about these types of reasons – get the right clothing, put baskets next to the door to hold hats and mittens, pack lunch the night before – in order to get our children outside.[70]

For other types of reasons, such as risk of harm to health, due to heat or cold, or risk of physical harm, due to high winds or lightning, we apply creativity to *do what we can* to spend time outdoors. This could look like having breakfast outdoors in the cool of the early morning, or taking advantage of an indoor nature center to learn and observe without the elements.

Take - Don't Send - Your Children Outside

The third and final step is to address the pushback many of us receive from our children about spending time outdoors. Here, Charlotte Mason gives more valuable advice: don't send your children outside but *take* them.[71] I will admit, this can be tough. At my house, I always have laundry to move around, dishes to wash, and something to clean or tidy. But to really get my kids settled outside, I *have* to go with them – at least for a bit. In fact, I usually lock the door on my way out and keep the key in my pocket, so that my boys don't try to sneak back in.

---

[70] Ibid.

[71] Ibid., 43.

For some families, time outdoors comes naturally. Their children crave it and happily spend hours playing in the garden making mud pies and building forts. Other families face more challenges, whether it's reluctant children, extreme weather, or simply lacking a habit of going outdoors. But wherever we fall on this spectrum, the goal is not to tick off the required number of hours spent outdoors each day. The goal is to be the type of family who prioritizes outdoor play appropriately and that encourages our children to build life-giving relationships with the natural world.

7

Education is a Life for You, Too

E ducation is not a destination any will reach in their lifetime. Many of us acknowledge this when we say that we want our children to grow up to be life-long learners. In fact, Charlotte Mason was concerned with the ability of adults to use their leisure time to continue learning and growing themselves. To this end, she says,

> Now, no one can employ leisure fitly whose mind is not brought into active play every day; the small affairs of a man's own life supply no intellectual food and but small and monotonous intellectual exercise. Science, history, philosophy, literature, must no longer be the luxuries of the 'educated' classes; all classes must be educated and sit down to these things of the mind as they do to their daily bread.[72]

Education is not just a life for our children. It's a life for *us* as well. In order to grasp the full richness of the Charlotte Mason philosophy, we must also see how it applies to ourselves, not just our children.

---

[72] Mason, *Philosophy*, 42.

Parents Are Also Born Persons

Charlotte Mason's philosophy begins with the premise that "Children are born persons".[73] If we take this to be true, it follows that we parents have never stopped being persons. In terms of education, this means that we have minds. Minds, as we see in Chapter Five, crave ideas just as the body craves food.

Charlotte Mason writes,

> *If you ever find yourself sinking to a dull, commonplace level, chances are you aren't reading, and therefore not thinking.*[74]

I often feel just that way: dull and commonplace. Life with children, especially young children, can often be repetitive, exhausting, and challenging. My mind is more often dazed and frazzled than a place of growth and vitality. This quote suggests, though, that the problem isn't my children, it's my neglect of my mind.

Mothers Require Living Ideas

If the minds of our children need a generous diet of living ideas in order to grow and sustain their mental life, then we, their parents, need the same.[75] If we stop eating, our bodies stop functioning properly. If we stop taking in ideas that prompt reflection, rumination, and deep thought, we shift into that numbed state. Our minds are starving.

---

[73] Charlotte Mason's Twenty Principles, Principle 1.

[74] Cholmondeley, *Story.*

[75] Charlotte Mason's Twenty Principles, Principle 8.

Whether you feel "dull and common place", "dazed and frazzled", or something else, these are all signs that our minds have stopped doing what they ought. They are no longer contemplating living ideas; therefore, they are not growing. Our responsibility, then, is to nourish our minds as we would our bodies, with regular meals of nutritious food.[76]

We sometimes encounter living ideas through our atmosphere. We watch those around us, speak with them, and receive inspiration. We may also find ideas in the natural world around us. However, we do not need to leave the nourishment of our minds completely to chance. We can seek ideas deliberately by reading living books.

Investing Time in Self-Education

We may not take in as many ideas as our children. We are not at leisure to spend as much time in study as they do. But we need to remember the principle: living ideas are vital, and that in order for us to keep our minds living and active, we need to feed them their appropriate measure.

In Charlotte Mason circles, this concept is called 'mother culture'. Charlotte Mason never used the expression herself, but an article of that name was published in the magazine she edited. Maybe you can relate to this quote from that article:

> So many mothers say, "I simply have no time for myself!" "I never read a book!" Or else, "I don't think it is right to think of myself!" They not only starve their minds, but they do it deliberately, and with a sense of self-sacrifice which seems to

---

[76] Ibid.

supply ample justification.[77]

It is all too easy to justify spending our time on activities other than mother culture. It can feel selfish to sit and read when there are so many other tasks that need doing. But as the author of the article says, when we don't make time for reading and learning, we are starving our minds. And as we stagnate, our children are growing and learning. The article compels us to consider what will happen when our children are older. They will need the counsel and experience of adults who have continued to learn, grow, and mature beyond their teens and early twenties.[78]

Pursuing the Life of Education Ourselves

The "Mother Culture" article encourages mothers to make a habit of reading for about thirty minutes a day. The books you choose should challenge you to think and meditate on the ideas they convey.

As we consider where to invest our precious time, we can take the same principles to heart that we use when choosing books for our children. We should choose books from all areas of knowledge: the knowledge of God, the knowledge of man, and the knowledge of the universe.[79] We should seek out books that are well-written, with ideas that make us think.[80] As we encounter these living ideas, our minds continue to live and grow.

---

[77] "Mother Culture", *The Parents' Review*, (Ambleside, Parents' National Educational Union, 1892/3), 92–95.

[78] Ibid.

[79] Mason, *Philosophy*, 254.

[80] Mason, *School Education*, 169.

If we are born persons, if we have minds that crave ideas the way bodies crave food, then the path before us begins to take shape. We acknowledge that we aren't already 'educated', but are still on the journey. We need an appropriate diet for our minds, and we need to set aside time to partake of the meal. Mother culture isn't superfluous or selfish, any more than taking time to eat your lunch. We are walking the same road as our children, just a little way ahead. Let's keep walking.

Continuing Your Charlotte Mason Journey

Education is an atmosphere, a discipline, and a life.

I hope that over the course of this book, you have been struck by the beauty of a Charlotte Mason education. Atmosphere, discipline, and life are tools that educate holistically. They address children's values, character, and intellect. They trust a child's intrinsic desire to learn, and avoid extrinsic rewards and punishments. This is how we can raise children who love to learn their entire lives.

These tools are rich, deep principles of education; yet, they are also practical and applicable. This is why I believe they make such an excellent starting point to the Charlotte Mason philosophy. Once we begin to grasp them, we can start using them immediately, even if we haven't read all the books or pored over curricula options.

Atmosphere, discipline, and life also serve as an excellent introduction to the Charlotte Mason philosophy as a whole. Within these tools, you see Charlotte Mason's heart for the education of children, particularly her desire to see the minds of children fed upon living ideas.[81] However, this is only an introduction and a beginning of a journey. Atmosphere, discipline, and life are merely three of Charlotte Mason's twenty principles. The next question, then, is, "Where to go from here?"

---

[81] Mason, *Philosophy*, 78.

With an appreciation of the 'how' to apply the Charlotte Mason principles, I believe the next best thing to do is to dig further into the 'why'. This book is no substitute for reading Charlotte Mason for yourself. She eloquently wrote about her educational philosophy, and her volumes are truly living books. They will give you many worthy ideas to meditate on, and will help you navigate your homeschooling journey.

With that in mind, I recommend reading one of her books as a next step. In *Towards a Philosophy of Education,* Charlotte Mason discusses her twenty principles and gives an overview of the areas of knowledge covered in her curriculum. If jumping into one of her volumes is overwhelming, you might consider reading a paraphrase in modern English, or *Mind to Mind* by Karen Glass. This book is *Philosophy of Education* with most of the cultural references removed, which can be difficult to understand and ultimately distracting from the content of the book.

If you aren't quite ready to read one of Charlotte Mason's complete volumes, another good option is to read a book that dives into all of her principles, not just her three principles of atmosphere, discipline, and life. I highly recommend *For the Children's Sake* by Susan Schaeffer Macaulay. This book is a seminal work in the Charlotte Mason sphere. It is also very accessible and goes over the philosophy thoroughly.

Finally, I have included a list of recommended reading at the end of this book. I have linked to articles, books, and resources that I have either referenced within this book or that are particularly relevant to atmosphere, discipline, and life.

Diving into educational philosophy is no small endeavor. I believe, though, that the pursuit of wisdom and understanding will bring that vitality of mind that Charlotte Mason wanted for all people.[82] I wish you all the best on your journey.

_____

82 Ibid.

Recommended Reading

Why Atmosphere, Discipline, and Life?

Towards a Philosophy of Education, Chapter Six, 'Three Instruments of Education'. Charlotte Mason.

Atmosphere

"The Atmosphere of the Home" . M. F. Jerrod, *The Parents' Review*. Ambleside: Parents' National Educational Union, 1897. Available from: https://www.amblesideonline.org/PR/PR08p772AtmosphereHome.shtml.

School Education, Chapter 3, 'Masterly Inactivity'. Charlotte Mason.

School Education, Chapter 4 , 'Some Rights of the Children as Persons'. Charlotte Mason.

The Self-Driven Child. William Stixrud and Ned Johnson.

Discipline

Home Education, Part III "Habit is Ten Natures". Charlotte Mason.

Atomic Habits. James Clear.

Life

Home Education, Part II "Out-of-Door Life for Children". Charlotte Mason.

Last Child in the Woods. Richard Louv.

"Mother Culture". *The Parents' Review.* Available from: https://www.amblesideonline.org/PR/PR03p092MotherCulture.shtml.

Continuing Your Journey

An Essay Towards a Philosophy of Education. Charlotte Mason.

Mind to Mind: An Essay Towards a Philosophy of Education. Charlotte Mason with Karen Glass.

For the Children's Sake. Susan Schaeffer Macaulay.

"Thinking Love" podcast. Available from: https://thinkinglove.education.

Bibliography

Cholmondeley, Essex. *The Story of Charlotte Mason*. Dent, 1960.

Clear, James. *Atomic Habits*. Random House Business, 2018.

Jerrod, M.F., "The Atmosphere of the Home", *The Parents' Review*. Ambleside: Parents' National Educational Union, 1897.

Lansbury, Janet. "The Real Reason Toddlers Push Limits", *Elevating Childcare*. 2013. Available at https://www.janetlansbury.com/2013/10/the-real-reasons-toddlers-push-limits/.

McLeod, Saul. "Pavlov's Dogs", *Simple Psychology*. 2018. Available at https://www.simplypsychology.org/pavlov.html.

Mason, Charlotte. *Formation of Character*. Living Books Press, 2017.

Mason, Charlotte. *Home Education*. Living Book Press, 2017.

Mason, Charlotte. *An Essay Towards a Philosophy of Education*. Living Book Press, 2017.

Mason, Charlotte. *Ourselves*. Living Book Press, 2017.

Mason, Charlotte. *School Education*. Living Book Press, 2017.

"Mother Culture", *The Parents' Review.* Ambleside:Parents' National Educational Union, 1892/3.

Schwartz, Sandi. "Helicopter Parenting", *The Gottman Institute*, 2018. Available at https://www.gottman.com/blog/helicopter-parenting-good-intentions-poor-outcomes/.

Siegel, Daniel J. and Payne Bryson, Tina. *No Drama Discipline.* London: Scribe, 2014.

Stixrud, William and Johnson, Ned. *The Thriving Child.* Penguin, 2018.

About the Author

Amy is a wife, a mom of three boys, and an American ex-pat living in the north-west of the UK. She holds an MA in Education and worked for a number of years in higher education before leaving the workforce to care for her children. Her hope for her children is that they grow to be curious, thoughtful, self-motivated problem solvers, who can teach themselves anything they want to know.

Amy shares the practical working-out of her parenting and education philosophies at her blog, Around the Thicket. She regularly writes about mother culture, parenting, and the Charlotte Mason philosophy of education.

You will also find her on the Thinking Love podcast, where she is a co-host on the show, chatting about Charlotte Mason, the early years, and more.

You can connect with me on:
- https://aroundthethicket.com
- https://thinkinglove.education

Also by Amy Fischer

For your next steps in your Charlotte Mason journey, consider these courses and conferences from the Thinking Love podcast hosts, Amy Fischer and Leah Martin.

Use code BEFORE20 for twenty percent off the registration fee of any course.

'Education is a Life' Course

What do you need to launch your Charlotte Mason homeschool?

Amy and Leah, think it is pretty simple: *practical instruction rooted in foundational ideas.* You'll find both in this four week course designed to get you up and running with the Charlotte Mason method.

Covering living books, curriculum, scheduling and planning, and teaching your child, start here to learn how to put the Charlotte Mason method in action.

Visit https://thinkinglove.education/life for more details.

Habit Training Workshop
Ready to make habit training a *habit?*

Habits: we all have them, for better or for worse. As mothers, we want to endow our children with habits that will help them, and not hinder them throughout their lives. But helping our children develop the right habits is not a task for the faint of heart. It is no surprise that we find ourselves discouraged and disappointed.

That's why we've developed a Habit Training workshop: to provide the framework, the accountability, and the encouragement needed to gain traction with habit training.

Visit *https://thinkinglove.education/habits* for more details.

Wise Beginnings
Your kids are precious. So is your time.

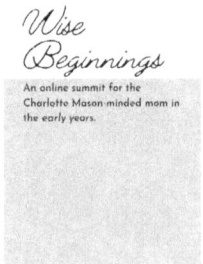

We know that the early years are flying by - along with a lot of your free time. *Wise Beginnings* is a live-or-later online summit focusing on the Charlotte Mason method for the early years, so you can fill up on what matters most to you right now. Featuring a keynote talk from Amber O'Neil Johnston (Heritage Mom blog), you'll be uplifted and empowered in your Charlotte Mason journey.

Visit *https://thinkinglove.education/wisebeginnings* for more details.

Printed in Great Britain
by Amazon